Harrison Ford

A Little Golden Book® Biography

By Kim Ostrow
Illustrated by Tim Jessell

A GOLDEN BOOK • NEW YORK

An imprint of Random House Children's Books • A division of Penguin Random House LLC
1745 Broadway, New York, NY 10019 • penguinrandomhouse.com • rhcbooks.com
Text copyright © 2025 by Kim Ostrow
Cover art and interior illustrations copyright © 2025 by Tim Jessell
Golden Books, A Golden Book, A Little Golden Book, the G colophon, and the distinctive
gold spine are registered trademarks of Penguin Random House LLC.
Library of Congress Control Number: 2024946518
ISBN 978-0-593-90012-3 (trade) — ISBN 978-0-593-90013-0 (ebook)
Manufactured in the United States of America
10 9 8 7 6 5 4 3 2 1
EU Contact: Penguin Random House Ireland, 32 Nassau Street, Dublin D02 YH68.
https://eu-contact.penguin.ie

Harrison Ford was born on July 13, 1942, in Chicago, Illinois. His parents met when they were both voice actors on the radio. After getting married, Harrison's father became an advertising executive. His mother stopped acting to raise Harrison and his brother, Terence.

Harrison was a quiet child. He liked taking care of his pet rats. He started out with two, but before long, there were baby rats running through Harrison's house. Some made their way outside and scampered around the neighborhood!

Harrison loved the outdoors. He joined the Boy
Scouts and wanted to be a forest ranger. At age fifteen,
he worked as an assistant counselor at a Boy Scout
camp, teaching campers what they needed to know to
earn their Reptile Study merit badge. That summer,
Harrison collected lots of snakes. He dug a big hole in
the ground so they'd have a cool place to live.

High school was challenging for Harrison. His grades weren't good, and he wasn't interested in sports or student council like the other kids. He didn't know where he fit in.

During his senior year, the school started a radio station. Like his parents before him, Harrison decided to give radio announcing a try. He became a sports broadcaster, calling all the school football games.

Harrison went on to study philosophy at Ripon College in Wisconsin, but he still struggled with schoolwork. He took a drama class because he thought it would be easy. What Harrison didn't realize was that he'd have to act in a play. He was so nervous that his legs shook—but he did it! Harrison decided that day to never let fear stop him from doing anything.

After college, Harrison stayed in Wisconsin to do summer stock theater. Being in plays and musicals made him happy. He loved that performing was a way to tell stories. Harrison began to think acting could be an interesting career.

He knew that most professional actors lived in New York or California. Unsure which place to move to, Harrison flipped a coin. New York won. But he decided he'd rather be somewhere warm and sunny. He tossed the coin one more time—Harrison Ford would be going to Hollywood!

In California, Harrison did odd jobs to pay his bills, like washing fishing boats and working as a late-night pizza chef. He also got cast in a show at the Laguna Playhouse.

One day, a talent scout saw the play and offered Harrison a contract with Columbia Pictures. He would be paid a small amount of money each week to do minor roles chosen by the movie studio.

In 1966, Harrison got his first movie role. He played a hotel bellhop in *Dead Heat on a Merry-Go-Round*. He only had two lines. Then, he acted in a few television shows, but he wasn't happy with the parts he was offered.

Harrison didn't give up on acting, but he did take a break. He wanted to accept roles because they sounded fun or interesting, not because he needed the work. It was time for a new plan.

Harrison decided to be a carpenter. He didn't know anything about carpentry—but that didn't stop him! He went straight to the public library, borrowed some textbooks, and taught himself. Soon, he was building beautiful doors, cabinets, and even a recording studio.

One of his clients was a casting director for a movie called *American Graffiti*, directed by George Lucas. He thought Harrison would be perfect for the film. He auditioned and got the role! The movie was a hit. Harrison knew he was making the right choice. He would keep working as a carpenter until more good acting roles came his way.

One morning, Harrison was putting away his tools
after installing a wooden door at a Hollywood producer's
office when George Lucas walked in. He was working on
a new movie called *Star Wars,* and asked Harrison to
read lines with the actors as they auditioned. After
hearing him act with more than one hundred people
that day, George realized that Harrison was perfect for
the part of Han Solo!

Star Wars came out in 1977. The film was a
worldwide sensation! And thirty-four-year-old Harrison
was a star! Fans loved watching the charming Han Solo
join forces with Luke Skywalker, Princess Leia, and
Chewbacca to defeat Darth Vader in this exciting
sci-fi movie.

The film was so popular they made many more! *Star Wars* would become one of the most successful franchises of all time. Harrison appeared as Han Solo in four sequels. First, in the 1980s, in *The Empire Strikes Back* and *Return of the Jedi,* and then again, more than thirty years later, in *The Force Awakens* and *The Rise of Skywalker.*

In 1981, Harrison was in another blockbuster movie. He played archaeologist Indiana Jones in *Raiders of the Lost Ark.* Indy was a brave adventurer, except when there were snakes and rats around! His character may have found them wiggly and scary, but Harrison—who grew up playing with rats and reptiles—did not. That, he says, is acting!

Harrison loved playing Indiana Jones. He did many of the stunts himself. He ran from a giant boulder, crossed a wobbly rope bridge, and was even dragged behind a truck for an exciting chase scene.

He would star in four more Indiana Jones movies: *The Temple of Doom, The Last Crusade, The Kingdom of the Crystal Skull,* and *The Dial of Destiny.* Harrison was seventy-nine years old—and still having fun—when he made the last action-packed film!

Throughout his career, Harrison starred in a variety of movies. He made comedies, thrillers, and love stories. In 1985, he was nominated for an Academy Award for Best Actor for his work in the dramatic film *Witness*. And he was the voice of a dog named Rooster in the 2019 animated film *The Secret Life of Pets 2*.

Acting and carpentry aren't Harrison's only skills—
he's also a pilot. He flies helicopters and small airplanes.

Just like when he was a Boy Scout, Harrison still
loves nature. He works with many groups to help the
environment and protect the rainforest. He lives on an
800-acre ranch in Jackson Hole, Wyoming, and he has
donated half of that land to a nature reserve.

Harrison Ford has been making movies for more than fifty years, playing some of the most popular characters in film history. His success didn't come quickly or easily, but he never gave up. Harrison loves acting. And audiences love watching him act, telling stories that take place on land, at sea, and in galaxies far, far away!